SAN FRANCISCO 49ERS

The NFL's Greatest Teams

Marcia Zappa

Big Buddy Books
An Imprint of Abdo Publishing
www.abdopublishing.com

www.abdopublishing.com

Published by Abdo Publishing, a division of ABDO, PO Box 398166, Minneapolis, Minnesota 55439.
Copyright © 2015 by Abdo Consulting Group, Inc. International copyrights reserved in all countries. No part
of this book may be reproduced in any form without written permission from the publisher. Big Buddy Books™
is a trademark and logo of Abdo Publishing.

Printed in the United States of America, North Mankato, Minnesota.
042014
092014

Cover Photo: ASSOCIATED PRESS.
Interior Photos: ASSOCIATED PRESS.

Coordinating Series Editor: Rochelle Baltzer
Contributing Editors: Bridget O'Brien, Sarah Tieck
Graphic Design: Michelle Labatt

Library of Congress Cataloging-in-Publication Data

Zappa, Marcia, 1985-
San Francisco 49ers / Marcia Zappa.
     pages cm. -- (The NFL's greatest teams)
     ISBN 978-1-62403-366-7
1. San Francisco 49ers (Football team)--History--Juvenile literature. I. Title.
   GV956.S3Z37 2015
   796.332'640979461--dc23
                                                           2013051244

Contents

A Winning Team

The San Francisco 49ers are a football team from San Francisco, California. They have played in the National Football League (NFL) for more than 60 years.

The 49ers have had good seasons and bad. But time and again, they've proven themselves. Let's see what makes the 49ers one of the NFL's greatest teams.

Red, gold, white, and black are the team's colors.

League Play

The NFL got its start in 1920. Its teams have changed over the years. Today, there are 32 teams. They make up two conferences and eight divisions.

The 49ers play in the West Division of the National Football Conference (NFC). This division also includes the Arizona Cardinals, the Saint Louis Rams, and the Seattle Seahawks.

Team Standings

The NFC and the American Football Conference (AFC) make up the NFL. Each conference has a north, south, east, and west division.

The Dallas Cowboys (*right*) and the Seattle Seahawks are rivals of the 49ers.

Fans get excited to watch their team play!

Kicking Off

The San Francisco 49ers started out in 1946. They were founded by Tony Morabito. The 49ers were one of the first teams in the All-America Football Conference (AAFC). In 1950, the 49ers joined the NFL after the AAFC stopped operating.

In 1849, thousands of people moved to Northern California looking for gold. They became known as 49ers. The football team is named for them.

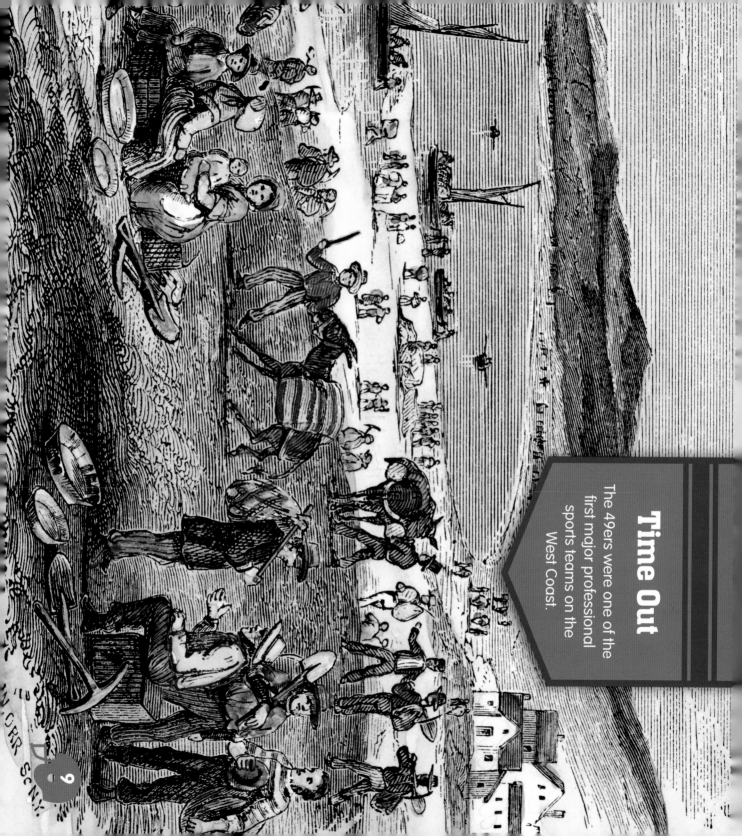

Time Out

The 49ers were one of the first major professional sports teams on the West Coast.

Highlight Reel

The 49ers struggled in their new league. They only made it to the play-offs once from the 1950s to the 1960s. In the early 1970s, they made it to the play-offs three times. But, the Dallas Cowboys beat them each time.

In 1977, Edward DeBartolo Jr. became the team's owner. He worked hard to make them stronger. In 1979, he hired Bill Walsh as head coach. Later that year, the team **drafted** quarterback Joe Montana.

Win or Go Home

NFL teams play 16 regular season games each year. The teams with the best records are part of the play-off games. Play-off winners move on to the conference championship. Then, conference winners face off in the Super Bowl!

Montana became known for his fourth-quarter comebacks. So, he was often called "Joe Cool" or "the Comeback Kid."

Walsh and Montana led the 49ers to several winning seasons in the 1980s. The team won its first Super Bowl in 1982. They won again in 1985 and 1989. Walsh **retired** in 1989. In 1990, the team won its fourth Super Bowl. The next year, Montana got hurt. Steve Young took his place. He led the 49ers to their fifth Super Bowl win in 1995.

The 49ers struggled in the 2000s. Finally in 2013, they returned to the Super Bowl. But, they lost to the Baltimore Ravens 34–31.

The NFC championship game in 1982 was close. During the last minute of the game, Montana threw a touchdown pass to Dwight Clark. This play is called "the Catch."

In the 1990 Super Bowl, the 49ers beat the Denver Broncos 55–10. That is the biggest win in Super Bowl history!

Halftime! Stat Break

Famous Coaches

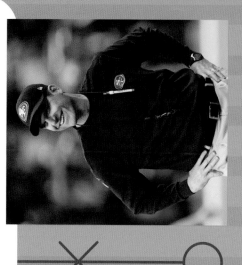

Bill Walsh (1979–1988)
Jim Harbaugh (2011–)

Pro Football Hall of Famers & Their Years with the 49ers

Fred Dean, Defensive End (1981–1985)
Jimmy Johnson, Cornerback (1961–1976)
Ronnie Lott, Cornerback/Safety (1981–1990)
Hugh McElhenny, Halfback (1952–1960)
Joe Montana, Quarterback (1979–1992)
Leo Nomellini, Defensive Tackle (1950–1963)
Joe Perry, Fullback (1948–1960, 1963)
Jerry Rice, Wide Receiver (1985–2000)
Bob St. Clair, Tackle (1953–1963)
Y.A. Tittle, Quarterback (1951–1960)
Bill Walsh, Coach (1979–1988)
Dave Wilcox, Linebacker (1964–1974)
Steve Young, Quarterback (1987–1999)

Championships

SUPER BOWL APPEARANCES: 1982, 1985, 1989, 1990, 1995, 2013

SUPER BOWL WINS: 1982, 1985, 1989, 1990, 1995

Team Records

RUSHING YARDS
Career: Frank Gore, 9,967 yards and gaining (2005–)
Single Season: Frank Gore, 1,695 yards (2006)

PASSING YARDS
Career: Joe Montana, 35,124 yards (1979–1992)
Single Season: Jeff Garcia, 4,278 yards (2000)

RECEPTIONS
Career: Jerry Rice, 1,281 receptions (1985–2000)
Single Season: Jerry Rice, 122 receptions (1995)

ALL-TIME LEADING SCORER
Jerry Rice, 1,130 points (1985–2000)

Fan Fun

NICKNAMES: The Niners, The Gold Rush, The Red and Gold

STADIUM: Levi's Stadium

LOCATION: Santa Clara, California

MASCOT: Sourdough Sam

Coaches' Corner

In 1979, Bill Walsh took over a struggling 49ers team. During his first season, the team won only two games. But by 1982, they were Super Bowl **champions**! Walsh led the team to two more Super Bowl wins. He **retired** in 1989.

Jim Harbaugh also joined the 49ers when they were down. He became the head coach in 2011. During his first season, he led them to the play-offs. The next year, he led them to the Super Bowl!

Jim Harbaugh (*right*) coached against his brother John (*left*) in the 2013 Super Bowl. John is the coach for the Baltimore Ravens.

Walsh made up the "West Coast Offense." This type of offense uses lots of fast, short passes.

Star Players

Joe Perry FULLBACK (1948–1960, 1963)

Joe "the Jet" Perry was known for his speed. In 1953 and 1954, he became the first NFL player to rush for 1,000 yards two seasons in a row. As a 49er, Perry had 8,689 rushing yards. Only Frank Gore has more.

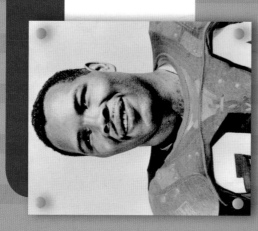

Y.A. Tittle QUARTERBACK (1951–1960)

Y.A. Tittle was an important member of the team's "Million Dollar Backfield." He and three others made up this powerful offense. Tittle was known as a strong quarterback.

18

Joe Montana QUARTERBACK (1979–1992)

Joe Montana led the 49ers to four Super Bowl wins. He was named the game's Most Valuable Player (MVP) three times. He was also the NFL's MVP twice. During his time with the team, Montana had 35,124 passing yards. That is more than any other 49er.

Ronnie Lott CORNERBACK/SAFETY (1981–1990)

Ronnie Lott was the team's first pick in the 1981 **draft**. His strong defensive play helped the 49ers make it to four Super Bowls. Lott has 63 **career interceptions**. Of these, 51 were for the 49ers. That is more than any other 49er.

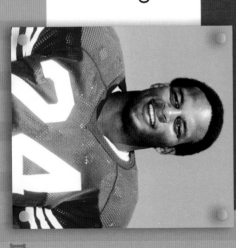

Jerry Rice WIDE RECEIVER (1985–2000)

Jerry Rice played for the 49ers for 16 seasons. He helped the team win three Super Bowls. He was named the game's MVP in 1989. When Rice **retired** from the NFL in 2004, he had 1,549 receptions and 208 touchdowns. That is more than any other player!

Steve Young QUARTERBACK (1987–1999)

Steve Young became the team's starting quarterback in 1991. In 1992 and 1994, he was named the NFL's MVP. Young led the 49ers to their fifth Super Bowl win in 1995. He threw a record six touchdowns in the game and was named MVP.

Colin Kaepernick QUARTERBACK (2011–)

Colin Kaepernick was **drafted** by the 49ers in 2011. The next year, he became the team's starting quarterback. Kaepernick rushed for 181 yards in one game. That is more than any other quarterback! And, he led the team to the 2013 Super Bowl.

Frank Gore RUNNING BACK (2005–)

Frank Gore joined the 49ers in 2005. He rushed for more than 1,000 yards during seven different seasons. By 2013, Gore had rushed for 9,967 total yards and 60 touchdowns. That is more than any other 49er.

Levi's Stadium

In 2014, the 49ers got a new stadium. Levi's Stadium is in Santa Clara, California. It can hold about 68,500 people.

Before this, the team played their home games at Candlestick Park in San Francisco. Candlestick Park opened in 1960. The 49ers began playing there in 1971.

Levi's Stadium started being built in 2012.

The 49ers played their last season in Candlestick Park in 2013.

The Niners

Many fans of the 49ers call them "the Niners." Others call them "the Gold Rush" or "the Red and Gold."

Sourdough Sam is the team's **mascot**. He wears blue jeans, gloves, a western hat, and a jersey with the number 49. Banjo Man has also appeared at home games to cheer on the team.

Fans cheer loudly when they see Sourdough Sam!

Banjo Man started appearing at home games in 1983. He plays the banjo!

Final Call

The San Francisco 49ers have a long, rich history. They ruled the NFL in the 1980s and early 1990s. Even during losing seasons, true fans have stuck with them. Many believe that the 49ers will remain one of the greatest teams in the NFL.

Fans of the 49ers are often called "the 49ers Faithful."

Through the Years

1969
Joe Perry and Leo Nomellini are the first 49ers in the Pro Football Hall of Fame.

1971
Candlestick Park becomes the team's home field. Before this, they played at Kezar Stadium.

1957
The 49ers play in their first NFL play-off game.

1950
The AAFC stops operating. The 49ers join the NFL.

1946
The 49ers play in the first season of the AAFC.

28

1979

Bill Walsh becomes the team's head coach.

1982

The 49ers play in their first Super Bowl. They beat the Cincinnati Bengals 26–21.

1990

Joe Montana is the first person to be named the Super Bowl's MVP three times.

1989

The 49ers win their third Super Bowl. They become known as "the Team of the 80s."

2013

The 49ers play in their sixth Super Bowl. They lose the game for the first time in team history.

Postgame Recap

1. Who was the coach of the San Francisco 49ers during their first three Super Bowl wins?
   A. Bill Walsh   **B.** Y.A. Tittle   **C.** Jim Harbaugh

2. What is the name of the stadium where the 49ers play their home games?
   A. Kezar Stadium   **B.** Candlestick Park   **C.** Levi's Stadium

3. Where is it located?
   A. San Francisco, California
   B. Santa Clara, California
   C. Los Angeles, California

4. Name 3 of the 13 49ers in the Pro Football Hall of Fame.

5. Which of these teams is a rival of the 49ers?
   A. The Green Bay Packers
   B. The New Orleans Saints
   C. The Dallas Cowboys

1. A.   2. C.   3. B.   4. See page 14   5. C.

Glossary

career work a person does to earn money for living.

champion the winner of a championship, which is a game, a match, or a race held to find a first-place winner.

draft a system for professional sports teams to choose new players. When a team drafts a player, they choose that player for their team.

interception (ihn-tuhr-SEHP-shuhn) when a player catches a pass that was meant for the other team's player.

mascot something to bring good luck and help cheer on a team.

retire to give up one's job.

Websites

To learn more about the NFL's Greatest Teams, visit **booklinks.abdopublishing.com**. These links are routinely monitored and updated to provide the most current information available.

31

Index